AR 36193 4.8 pts 0.5 = ½

LINCOLN SCHOOL LIBRARY
410 W. 157th Street
Calumet City, Illinois
708-862-6620

P9-DXR-418

# Maps and Our World

T 7250

**Text:** Robert Coupe

**Consultant:** Colin Sale, Geography Lecturer and Author

This edition first published 2003 by

**MASON CREST PUBLISHERS INC.**

370 Reed Road

Broomall, PA 19008

All rights reserved. No part of this publication may be reproduced
or transmitted in any form or by any means, electronic or mechanical,
including photocopying, recording, taping, or any information storage and
retrieval system, without permission in writing from the publisher.

© Weldon Owen Inc.

Conceived and produced by

**Weldon Owen Pty Limited**

Library of Congress Cataloging-in-Publication Data
on file at the Library of Congress
ISBN: 1-59084-175-1

Printed in Singapore.
1 2 3 4 5 6 7 8 9 06 05 04 03

# CONTENTS

# OUR WORLD

Maps can tell us a lot about our world. They can be used to show many things. They can tell us about different countries, their environments, and climates. They can tell us about rivers, lakes, mountains, and oceans. They can tell us about how people use the world, its natural resources, its animals, plants, and even tell us about other people. Maps can also show us how to find our way.

NORTH AMERICA

PACIFIC OCEAN

**World Environments**
The Earth's environments are closely related to its climate zones. This map shows the many kinds of environments around the world.

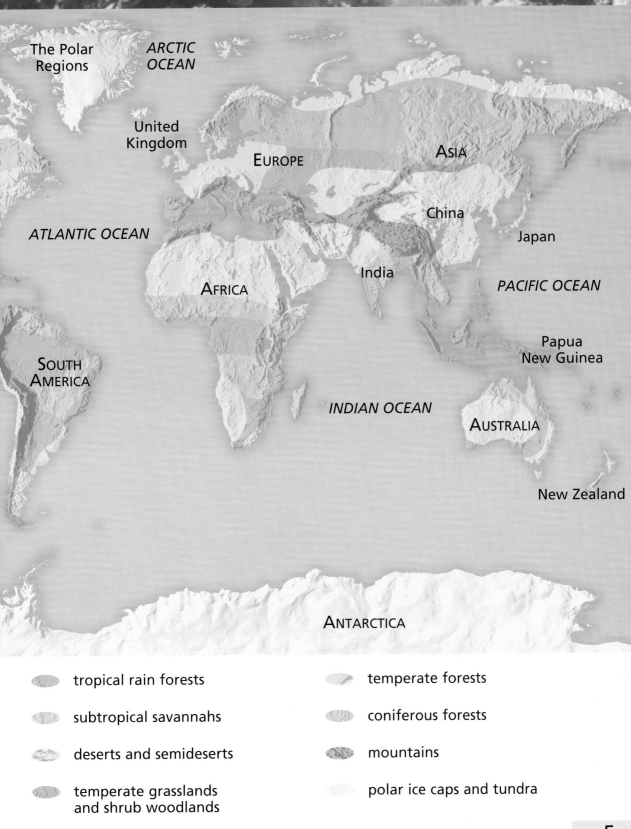

The Polar Regions

ARCTIC OCEAN

United Kingdom

EUROPE

ASIA

China

Japan

ATLANTIC OCEAN

AFRICA

India

PACIFIC OCEAN

SOUTH AMERICA

Papua New Guinea

INDIAN OCEAN

AUSTRALIA

New Zealand

ANTARCTICA

tropical rain forests

temperate forests

subtropical savannahs

coniferous forests

deserts and semideserts

mountains

temperate grasslands and shrub woodlands

polar ice caps and tundra

## Tropical Rain Forests

More animals and plants live in hot, wet forests than in any other environment.

## Savannahs

Savannahs are covered with grasses but have few trees. The African savannah is home to billions of animals.

# ENVIRONMENTS

There are many different environments on Earth. Climate and weather patterns help to create different environments. The animals and plants that live in a particular environment have adapted to live there successfully. Most of the environments shown on this page are found in hot climates. Some are very wet, and some are dry and have little rain.

**Deserts**

Deserts are dry places, but some animals and plants are able to live there. Cactus plants prefer deserts.

**Oceans**

Fish of all shapes and sizes live in the oceans. So do mammals such as whales and seals. Some fish and sea plants have brilliant colors.

The environments shown here are in parts of the world where the climate is temperate or cold. Temperate means a climate that is neither very hot nor very cold. In cold environments, many of the animals have thick fur. Some have thick layers of fat for extra warmth. In the coldest environments, only a few kinds of plants are able to grow.

**Temperate Forests**
Temperate forests have trees that need lots of rain. In some forests, trees have leaves all year round. In others they shed their leaves every autumn.

**Temperate Grasslands**
There is little shelter in grasslands, so some animals dig burrows underground. Grasslands are good hunting places for eagles and other birds of prey.

## Coniferous Forests

Pine trees are called conifers. They grow in areas where winters are cold and often snowy.

## Mountains

High mountain areas can be cold and windy.

## Polar Regions

The ice caps around the Arctic Ocean are bitterly cold. Most of the animals that live in these areas, such as polar bears and foxes, have thick fur.

## Filling Our Needs

As you can see, some parts of the Earth have many more resources than others.

 major gas fields

 major coal fields

 major oil fields

 urban areas such as towns, cities, and industries

 areas with large farms for growing crops and raising animals

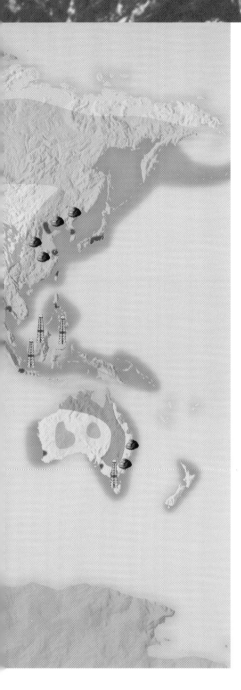

# FROM THE EARTH

The way people use the Earth to produce food and other materials can be shown on a map. Natural resources are the things that people use from the Earth. Resources such as crops and fish are called renewable resources, because they can grow again. Others cannot be renewed. We cannot renew some of the resources we use for energy, such as coal and oil.

areas with small farms where people grow crops and raise animals

deserts and dry grasslands where small numbers of animals graze

forested areas with some farming, hunting, and mining resources

grasslands where many animals graze

areas that are too cold or dry for farming

major fishing grounds

## WATER CYCLE

The Sun's heat turns seawater to vapor, which rises. When air carrying vapor rises, it is quickly cooled and changes into drops of water that form clouds. The water falls from the clouds as rain or snow and runs back into the sea. We call this process the water cycle.

## Oil and Gas

These form in rocks below the land or sea. We get them out by drilling.

## Uranium

Uranium is mined under the ground. In some countries it is used to make electricity.

## Geothermal Power

This is power we get from steam that comes out of the ground.

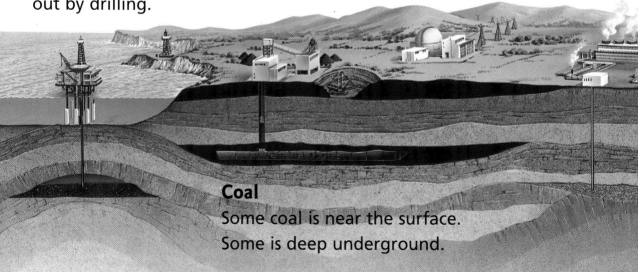

## Coal

Some coal is near the surface. Some is deep underground.

Energy is the power we need to make electricity and to run machines and factories. Most of our energy comes from natural resources such as oil, gas, and coal that will one day be used up. People are now using other sources of energy that will never run out. Some of these have another great advantage—they do not create pollution.

### Hydroelectric Power
In many countries, water stored in huge dams is released to make electricity.

### Wind Power
Windmills can change wind power into electricity.

### Solar Power
Special panels catch heat from the Sun and create electric power.

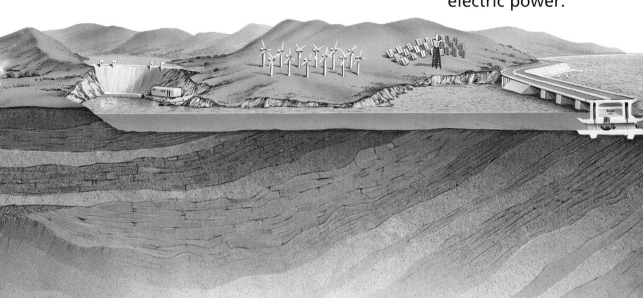

# Maps and Scales

A map is a drawing of the Earth, or a part of it, looking down from above. It might be of the whole world, or it might show a single country, or a tiny part of that country. Every map has a scale. The scale tells you how big the things that are shown on the map really are. The map on pages 4 and 5 is a small-scale map, because the whole world is drawn very small to fit on two pages.

### Amazing!

The word "atlas" comes from an ancient Greek myth. Atlas was a giant who started a war against the gods. The gods punished him by making him carry the world on his shoulders. The very first map books had a picture of Atlas carrying the world. Now we call a map book an "atlas."

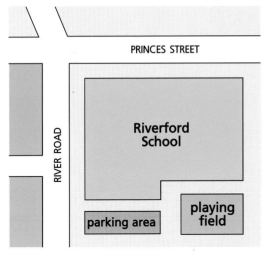

## Very Large Scale

This map is like a close-up of Riverford School. It could be useful, for example, to show visitors where they could park their cars.

## Large Scale

This map does not show the school in as much detail as the very large scale map. It shows us more information about the area around the school.

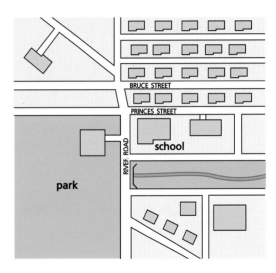

## Small Scale

This map could be useful if you wanted to travel from Portville or Barton to Riverford. But you would need a large-scale map, such as a street directory, to find the school.

# MAKE YOUR OWN MAP

People who make maps are called cartographers. Could you make a map of the area where you live? Think about the streets and buildings near your house. You will need to know their names and their positions. Are there any other features in your area, such as a river or a lake, that you might want to include? Think about the scale of your map. You might decide that large trees should be included, but bushes are too small and can be left out.

1 Begin by walking around your neighborhood. Draw a rough draft of the streets and the main features of the area.

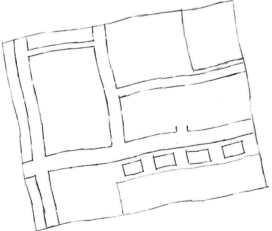

2 Use the correct scale by showing which street blocks are long and which are short.

**3** Write in the street names, and add all the buildings and other features you want to include. Imagine the shapes that things like buildings, parks, and rivers would have if you looked at them from above.

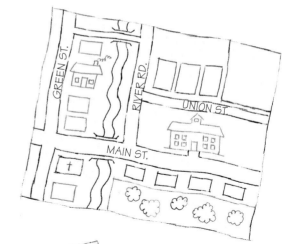

**4** Color your map. Use different colors for different kinds of places. Then list all the colors you used and write down what each color represents. This is called a key.

# MAPPING THE WORLD

How can a round world be shown on a flat map? If you peeled off a map printed on a globe, you would get pieces like these on the right. To make a flat map, the countries at the bottom and top of the globe are stretched out to fill in the gaps.

**What's the Time?**

The Sun shines on different parts of the world at different times. When it is noon in Greenwich, England, it is only 7 o'clock the same morning in the eastern United States. This map shows the different time zones around the world.

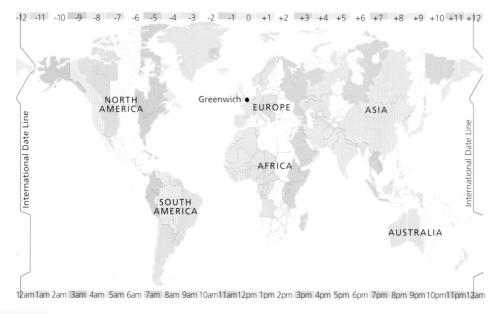

-12 -11 -10 -9 -8 -7 -6 -5 -4 -3 -2 -1 0 +1 +2 +3 +4 +5 +6 +7 +8 +9 +10 +11 +12

NORTH AMERICA
Greenwich •
EUROPE
ASIA
International Date Line
AFRICA
International Date Line
SOUTH AMERICA
AUSTRALIA

12am 1am 2am 3am 4am 5am 6am 7am 8am 9am 10am 11am 12pm 1pm 2pm 3pm 4pm 5pm 6pm 7pm 8pm 9pm 10pm 11pm 12am

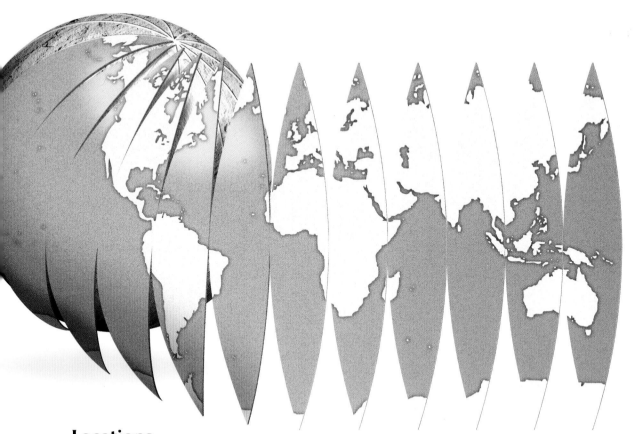

## Locations

Maps of the world are marked with two sets of lines. Lines of latitude go across the map, and lines of longitude go down the map.

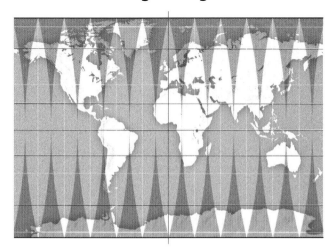

Arctic Circle

Tropic of Cancer

Equator

Tropic of Capricorn

Antarctic Circle

Greenwich Meridian

# READING A MAP

Most maps can show you how far one place is from another. Some maps can also tell you whether a place is hilly or flat, or if there are forests or deserts there. Different maps are designed to give you different information about a country or a region.

**Where Is It?**
Maps in atlases and street directories have a grid of lines to help you find the place you are looking for. If you look up the name of a place in the back of an atlas, it will tell you the page number of the map you need, and the grid lines it is closest to on the map.

# USING A SCALE

How far is it from Sydney to Perth? How long is the Darling River? Here's how you can use the scale to find out.

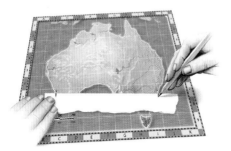

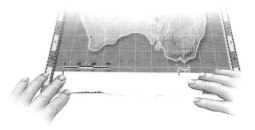

1 Hold the top edge of a strip of paper under the dots that show Sydney and Perth. Mark the dots on the paper.

2 Place the paper under the scale and line up the Perth dot next to 0. Mark where the scale ends and then move this mark to 0 again. Do this again until you reach the Sydney dot. Add up the distances.

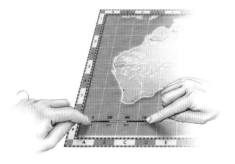

1 To measure the Darling River, bend a piece of string along the river on the map, from where it starts on the coast to where it ends.

2 Now straighten out the string and hold it along the scale. You can now figure out how long the river is.

## Compass

The compass on the map shows the four main directions— north, south, east, and west.

## North-northwest

A detailed compass can show even more directions. Did you know that north-northwest is between north and northwest?

## Scale

You can use the scale to figure out how far one place is from another.

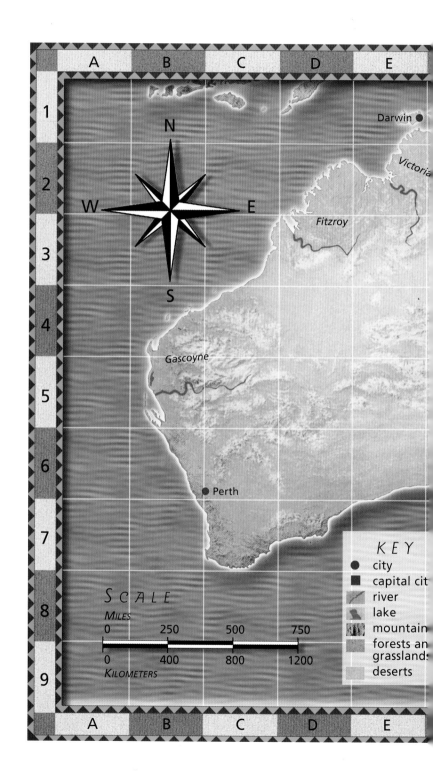

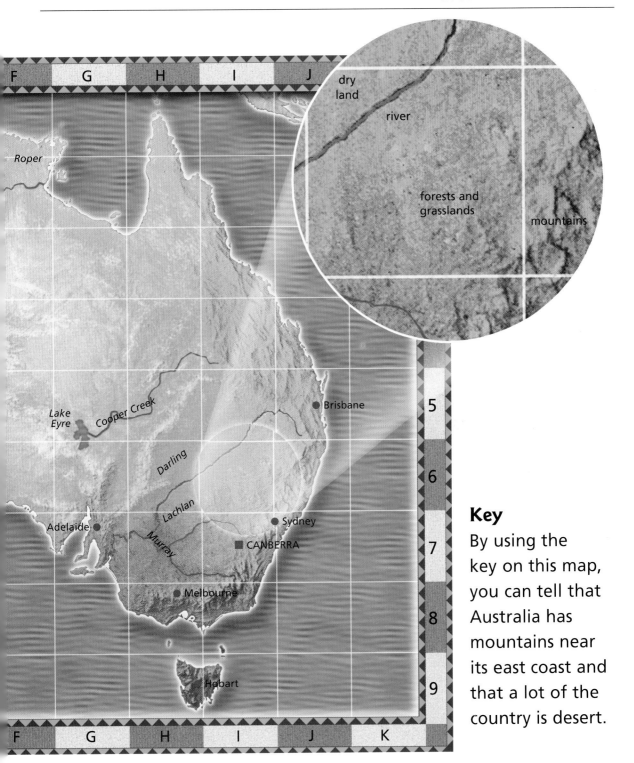

F  G  H  I  J

dry
land

river

Roper

forests and
grasslands

mountains

Lake
Eyre

Cooper Creek

●Brisbane

5

Darling

6

Lachlan

Adelaide ●

Murray

● Sydney

7

■ CANBERRA

● Melbourne

8

Hobart

9

F  G  H  I  J  K

**Key**

By using the
key on this map,
you can tell that
Australia has
mountains near
its east coast and
that a lot of the
country is desert.

# THE HUMAN FAMILY

Can you imagine a number as large as 6 billion? Almost that number of people now live on the Earth. Some countries have many people in a small area. We say these countries are densely populated. Others have fewer people in a large area. These countries are sparsely populated.

**Millions of People**

These are the countries with the biggest populations. There are more people in China than any other country in the world.

| China | India | U.S.A. | Indonesia | Brazil | Russia |
|---|---|---|---|---|---|
| 1.2 billion | 937 million | 264 million | 204 million | 161 million | 150 million |

Every second of every day, three babies are born. The world's population is growing much faster than ever before. Fifty years ago there were only about half as many people as there are today. It is no wonder that many parts of the world are getting overcrowded.

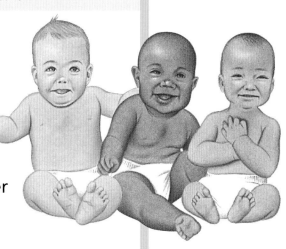

**Languages**
More than 3,000 languages are spoken around the world. This is how you say "hello" in four of the main ones.

*hello*
English
(350 million speakers)

*hola*
*o-la*
Spanish
(250 million speakers)

مرحبا
*mar-ha-ban*
Arabic
(150 million speakers)

你好
*ni hao*
Chinese
(1 billion speakers)

| Pakistan | Bangladesh | Japan | Nigeria |
|---|---|---|---|
| 132 million | 128 million | 126 million | 101 million |

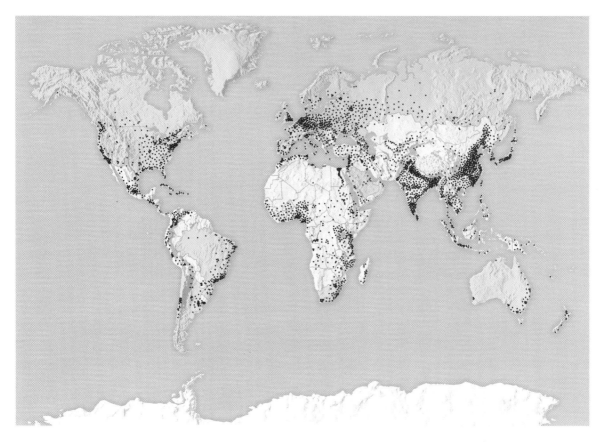

these areas contain the richer, developed countries

these areas contain the poorer, developing countries

In developed countries, most people live comfortably and have enough money for food and housing. In developing countries, many people are poor and their lives are very difficult. The red areas of this map show the parts of the world that are densely populated.

## More
Developed countries are richer and use more energy than developing countries, but they are less crowded.

## Less
Developing countries are poorer. They are more crowded, but they use less than half as much energy.

### DID YOU KNOW?

This graph shows how the world's population has grown in the last 300 years, and how it will probably grow in the next century. The number of people in developing countries is growing very fast. The number of people in developed countries is no longer growing at all.

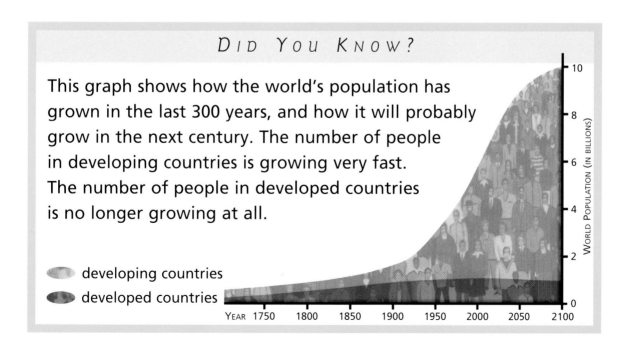

developing countries
developed countries

YEAR 1750  1800  1850  1900  1950  2000  2050  2100

WORLD POPULATION (IN BILLIONS)
10
8
6
4
2
0

# DANGER SIGNS

Environments change over time. Natural changes happen slowly, often over thousands of years. Yet in the past 200 years, many environments have been changed and damaged by the way people have treated them.

## Spreading Deserts

In some places, deserts are getting larger as people clear land for farming and then do not take care of the soil.

## Shrinking Forests

Imagine a world without trees. In some places, huge areas of forests are rapidly being cut down.

## DID YOU KNOW?

Trees in Brazil, in South America, are being cut down so quickly that every minute more than 7 acres (3 hectares) of rain forest are destroyed. As a result, many animals no longer have anywhere to live.

## Poisonous Rain

Chemicals in the air can turn rainwater into a weak acid. This can kill most plants.

## Dirty Air

Automobiles and factories make the air in some places unhealthy to breathe.

## Spoiled Water

Waste from factories and homes ends up in rivers and oceans. Some rivers are so polluted that fish no longer live in them.

# Glossary

**climate**  The pattern of weather that occurs in a place over a long period of time.

**compass**  In an atlas, this is an instrument that shows in which direction places are on the map.

**conifers**  Trees that have needlelike leaves all year round, and whose seeds are contained in hard cones.

**environment**  The natural surroundings of a place.

**equator**  An imaginary line around the world that lies halfway between the North and South Poles.

**Greenwich Meridian**  An imaginary straight line running from the North Pole to the South Pole and passing through Greenwich, an area near London, in England.

**lines of latitude**  Lines on a map that show how far a place is to the north or south of the equator.

**lines of longitude**  Lines on a map that show how far a place is to the east or west of the Greenwich Meridian.

**rain forests**  Dense forests that grow in very wet areas. Most of the world's rain forests are in warm tropical regions.

# INDEX

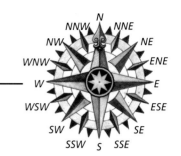

# PICTURE AND ILLUSTRATION CREDITS

[t=top, b=bottom, l=left, r=right, c=center, F=front, B=back, C=cover, bg=background]

**Susana Addario** 1c, 14br. **Ad Libitum/Michal Kanewski** 16bl. **Andrew Beckett /illustration** 28–29bc. **Jocelyne Best** 18bl. **Digital Stock** 4–32 borders, Cbg. **Digital Wisdom** 4–5c, 10–11c. **Chris Forsey** 12–13bc. **Ray Grinaway** 2l, 24–25lc, 27tl, 27tr. **Tim Hayward** 6–7c, 8–9c. **Stuart McVicar** 22tl, 22–23c, 19tc, 19bl, 26tc, 30tr. **Oliver Rennert** 12tl, 21tl, 21tr, 21bl, 21br. **Marco Sparaciari** 3tr, 25tr. **Sharif Tarabay/illustration** 20bl, FCc. **Thomas Trojer** 29tr, 30bc. **Weldon Owen** 15tl, 15cr, 15bl, 16–17rc, 27bc. **Amanda Woodward** 25c.

# BOOKS IN THIS SERIES